# FACING fear

## FINDING REFUGE IN THE GOD OF PEACE

PRESENTED TO

---

BY

---

DATE

---

Lifeway Press®
Brentwood, Tennessee

ISBN 978-1-0877-8495-3
Item 005842367
Dewey Decimal Classification Number: 242
Subject Heading: DEVOTIONAL LITERATURE / BIBLE STUDY AND TEACHING / GOD

Printed in the United States of America.

Student Ministry Publishing
Lifeway Resources
200 Powell Place, Suite 100
Brentwood, Tennessee 37027

We believe that the Bible has God for its author; salvation for its end; truth, without any mixture of error, for its matter; and that all Scripture is totally true and trustworthy. To review Lifeway's doctrinal guideline, please visit https://www.lifeway.com/about/doctrinal-guidelines.



---

# publishing team

*Director, Next Gen Ministry*
Chuck Peters

*Manager, Small Group Resources*
Karen Daniel

*Writer*
Zachary Ethridge

*Content Editor*
Kyle Wiltshire

*Production Editor*
April-Lyn Caouette

*Cover Design*
Grace Morgan

*Graphic Designer*
Shiloh Stufflebeam

# TABLE OF CONTENTS

# INTRO

We don't have to look very hard to see that our enemy, Satan, tries to overwhelm us with fear. We are constantly surrounded by painful trials, the threat of social rejection, and the many worries associated with life in the modern world. If we aren't careful and proactive, we can make a lifestyle out of worry. Where do we turn with all these fears?

Interestingly enough, the most repeated command in the Bible is "Fear not." Often, we see this as a demand, but it's more of an invitation. God's Word offers us freedom from the fears that can paralyze our lives. Again and again, God shows us the many reasons we can face our uncertain future with courage.

As we walk through these thirty days, we will discover that God's Word is full of promises for His children. Although we live in a scary and fallen world and may face uncertain and terrifying situations, God has not left us alone. On the contrary, as His Word reminds us: He is with us. He is our refuge in every season of life. There is nothing we can face that is beyond His reach.

As we look to Scripture throughout this book, we'll discover the ways in which God has been faithful to His people throughout all generations. God's people have faced all kinds of challenges and trials and their enemies have been fierce and evil, but God gave them peace in even the hardest times. Our God never changes. The One who was a fortress for David, Paul, and many others will be your rock as well when the storms come. You can face your fears with the God of peace by your side. Let's seek Him together in whatever you face in the season ahead.

# GETTING STARTED

This devotional contains thirty days of content, broken down into sections. Each day is divided into three elements—**discover**, **delight**, and **display**—to help you grow in your faith.

## DISCOVER

This section helps you examine the Bible in light of who God is and determine what it says about your identity in relationship to Him. Included here is the daily Scripture reading and key verses, along with illustrations and commentary to guide you as you learn more about God's Word.

## DELIGHT

In this section, you'll be challenged by questions and activities that help you see how God is alive and active in every detail of His Word and your life.

## DISPLAY

Here's where you take action. This section calls you to apply what you've learned through each day.

**Each day also includes a prayer activity at the conclusion of the devotion.**

**Throughout the devotional, you'll also find extra items to help you connect with the topic personally, such as Scripture memory verses and interactive articles.**

SECTION 1

# 10 THINGS TO KNOW ABOUT FEAR

*There are some things the Bible encourages us not to fear, such as Satan, people, and hardships. But we should fear the Lord. To fear the Lord is to respect His authority in every element of our lives, and over the next ten days, we will learn ten things about fear that will help us.*

DAY 1

# How to Fear the Lord

READ PSALM 111.

*The fear of the LORD is the beginning of wisdom; all who follow his instructions have good insight. His praise endures forever.*
*— Psalm 111:10*

## DISCOVER

When you think about the word "fear," what comes to mind? Anxiety, stress, worry, danger? Psalm 111:10 may be confusing if you read it with our typical understanding of fear. Here, the word means to be in awe, to be amazed, or to have a deep respect for something. This means, according to the psalmist, that the first step to wisdom is to be filled with wonder and respect for God.

Typically, the link between fear and wisdom isn't obvious. When we're scared, it often leads to either panic or paralysis. But the fear of the Lord—reverence and respect for Him—*does* lead to wisdom. Since we all need wisdom, all of us should be growing in the fear of the Lord. But how do we do this?

Look back through Psalm 111. When God's perfection comes into view, we cannot help but be in awe of Him. We will fear the Lord when we study His great works, (see v. 2), consider His majesty (see v. 3), remember His grace and compassion (see v. 4), and acknowledge His power (see v. 6). God is faithful, righteous, true, and trustworthy. To know Him is to be filled with wonder.

God's glory is most clearly seen in the face of Jesus. The God who reigns above all has looked down on you with great love. He has carried your sins and sorrows. He has risen in power. How awe-inspiring are His works! May a fresh sight of Him fill you with wonder and cause the fears that plague you to fade away in the light of His glory.

## DELIGHT

**Why may our unhealthy fears (such as FOMO, fear of rejection, and so on) lead to foolish thoughts or actions?**

**How can a bigger view of God shrink your fears?**

**What can you do to grow in your fear of the Lord?**

## DISPLAY

Psalm 111 begins and ends with praise (see Ps. 111:1,10). In other parts of Scripture, the fear of the Lord is often connected to worship (see Deut. 6:13; 1 Sam. 12:24; Rev. 15:4). In other words, one way you can grow in your reverence for God is through praising and worshiping Him. Fill your heart and mind with songs that lift up Jesus and remind you of His awesome works. Love Him with all your heart, worship Him with all your soul, and obey Him with all your strength—this is the fear of the Lord (see Deut. 10:12).

**Lord Jesus, I cannot even express how awesome You are. I worship You simply for who You are. I give You praise for all the things You have done. Fill my heart with holy fear for You until there is no more room for other fears. In Jesus's name, Amen.**

## DAY 2

# How Much You're Worth

READ MATTHEW 10:26-31.

*"So don't be afraid; you are worth more than many sparrows."*
*— Matthew 10:31*

## DISCOVER

Jesus warned His disciples that the world would mistreat them just as He had been mistreated (see Matt. 10:24-25). They would experience physical violence, social rejection, and verbal slander. But after sharing that difficult news, Jesus comforted them with these verses. He reminded them that nothing is hidden from God. He knows the truth—regardless of how others treat or perceive you.

People can harm us, but not forever, because God is the judge over all and He will have the final word. People can kill the body, but not our souls. Jesus lifts our heads above the present life to our eternal hope. You are on the winning side, so press on to live for Jesus. Shine His light, even when the darkness seeks to intimidate you. Satan and those who join him in opposing the Lord may hate you, but your heavenly Father loves you. Jesus wants you to remember that God knows the details of our lives and is in control over events and circumstances, big and small.

Therefore, do not be afraid. The pain of the present will give way to eternal promises. The present darkness will be undone by eternal light. The One who holds eternity also holds you, and you are more valuable to Him than many sparrows.

## DELIGHT

**What fears attempt to keep you from living for Jesus?**

**How important and helpful is it to your faith to understand that living like Jesus may bring opposition?**

**Does it comfort you to see God as both Judge and Father? Why or why not?**

## DISPLAY

Jesus says to not fear three different times in these verses. We shouldn't fear how people may treat us for our faith. God loves us and is overseeing the details our lives. But in the middle of all that, Jesus also says that there's something we *should* fear. He says we should "fear him who is able to destroy both soul and body in hell" (Matt. 10:28). In other words, we ought to tremble at the thought of being cut off from God. Man's rejection is temporary, but living for people rather than God has eternal consequences. Fear the Lord rather than humans and live for eternity. Journal your thoughts and feelings on how this truth makes you feel. Reflect on how you can live in reverent awe of God instead of in fear of the enemy.

**Heavenly Father, please give me courage today to live for You. Despite the intimidation and anger of the world, help me to overcome every fear. I trust that Your love for me is greater than any fear I may experience. In Jesus's name, Amen.**

## DAY 3

# His Love Is Perfect

READ 1 JOHN 4:7-21.

*There is no fear in love; instead, perfect love drives out fear, because fear involves punishment. So the one who fears is not complete in love.*
*— 1 John 4:18*

## DISCOVER

Many Christians struggle to experience the assurance of their salvation and may at times wonder if they are truly saved. We fear the judgment of God—rightly so—and we long for the confidence that we have eternal life. One of the main reasons John wrote this letter is to give believers assurance of their salvation. In these verses, John focuses on the assurance that comes from being transformed by God's love.

God loved us by sending Jesus to die for us. When we receive His gift of love—Jesus—He gives us the Holy Spirit, and when the Spirit comes to dwell within our hearts, He begins to make us more like Jesus. We grow in our love for others. We love people in word and through our actions. When we can see God's love at work in and through us toward other people, this is evidence that God has saved us. God's love working in and through us gives us assurance that we are truly His.

We might feel a looming sense of fear because of the judgment that will come when Jesus returns. But Christ has rescued believers from the final judgment. We are forgiven forever because of what Jesus did on the cross. May God's verdict of forgiveness drive out fear and fill you with the assurance of His love.

## DELIGHT

**Have you ever struggled with assurance of your salvation? If so, why?**

**How have you combated those struggles?**

**What did you learn from today's Scripture reading that can help you in the future?**

## DISPLAY

The primary way we find assurance is through Jesus Himself. But the apostle John also explains that a secondary way to find assurance is through our own spiritual transformation. When you see God's love working in your life, changing your heart and making you more like Jesus, you will feel a confidence in your salvation. The fruit of your life reveals the genuineness of the roots, showing that you are truly His. If you want to experience assurance, it is critical that you love in word and in deed. Put God's love into action today.

Reflect on your life before you followed Jesus and how it has changed since you've come to faith in Him. Answer the questions below to help you reflect.

**What did my life before Jesus look like?**

**In what ways has His love begun to transform me?**

**Lord Jesus, thank You for loving me. Help me love others as You have first loved me. I want my life to show that I belong to You. I cannot do it myself, but I know You can do it in me. I receive and desire to give Your love today. Amen.**

## DAY 4

# No More Shame

READ GENESIS 3.

*And he said, "I heard you in the garden, and I was afraid because I was naked, so I hid."*
*— Genesis 3:10*

## DISCOVER

We all know the fear that comes from having a guilty conscience. When we know we've made the wrong choice, we often feel deeply anxious. The fear of getting caught, being embarrassed, or facing the consequences can compel us to hide. God made us to be moral creatures—we can't escape the way that He has made us to sense right from wrong.

Adam and Eve experienced this kind of fear in the garden. After eating the fruit from the tree that God had forbidden, they immediately knew they had sinned and felt the piercing guilt of their failure. Their physical exposure corresponded to the spiritual nakedness they felt before God. In fear, they tried to hide themselves.

God didn't make us for sin—He created us to live in His goodness. The fear and shame that comes from sin isn't what God wants for us. Sin brings guilt, but that guilt should drive us *to* God, not away from Him. He is the only one who can wash our sins away and cleanse our conscience from guilt and shame. When fear compels us to hide from God, Satan wins. But when we walk into the light of God's grace, the fear of judgment is removed and we experience the joy of forgiveness and peace with God.

## DELIGHT

**Where do you turn when you know you've messed up?**

**Whom can you be totally honest with in your life?**

**How can you overcome fear and shame from past sins?**

## DISPLAY

The fear and shame of a guilty conscience is something that every person has faced. But you don't have to stay stuck in that guilt—you can experience true forgiveness and freedom through Jesus. One of the best ways to find a way forward is to talk to someone about it. When sin remains hidden, we give Satan ammunition to use against our spirits. But something powerful happens when we confess our sins to others: we experience God's love and grace through their support. God is ready to extend mercy the moment we turn to Him. Experience His cleansing grace today—pray about who you can talk to, then seek out the trusted mentor or friend whom God leads you to and confess your sin.

**Father, I know that I have made many mistakes. I confess my sins to You today and ask You to give me the peace of Your forgiveness. Please wash, renew, and restore me through Your grace. In Jesus's name, Amen.**

## DAY 5

# Comfort in the Valley

READ PSALM 23.

*Even when I go through the darkest valley, I fear no danger, for you are with me; your rod and your staff — they comfort me.*
*— Psalm 23:4*

## DISCOVER

There's a reason that Psalm 23 is one of the most well-known parts of the Bible. This psalm has offered comfort and strength to believers throughout history. It's a reminder of God's constant care for His children. In the green pastures and in the darkest valleys, Jesus is with you.

When my kids go to bed, sometimes one of them accidentally forgets something downstairs. They're afraid to go downstairs by themselves at night, but their fears are gone when I walk with them through the dark house. My presence is a source of peace for them. The darkness may be scary for them, but they know they are safe with me. They know I love them and will take care of them.

The dark valleys of life are certainly frightening. We don't have to pretend that life isn't scary sometimes or act like the valleys aren't truly dark. Notice that David didn't find peace by pretending that the valley wasn't that bad or by putting a positive spin on the situation. He acknowledged that he was often in real danger from King Saul and others who were seeking to harm him. But no matter who was against him, David knew that the Lord was with him. That is what helped eliminate his fear.

## DELIGHT

**What are you afraid of in this season of your life?**

**What makes you feel safe?**

**How can you find peace in God's presence?**

…s us to keep marching ahead through the valleys. Satan …eat. He wants us to give up and quit. But God is leading …ewhere—the valley isn't the final destination. Know that He …u. Jesus is the Good Shepherd, and with Him, you can make it …n the darkest of valleys.

…f you ever feel like you want to throw in the towel, talk to someone who loves you. You were never made to go through these things alone—God has placed people in your life to help you. God is with you, and other believers will be, too, as you navigate the difficult seasons ahead.

**Lord, thank You for Your constant love and care. I know that You are with me through the best and worst times. Help me to feel Your presence, even when I am afraid. Please calm my fears. In Jesus's name, Amen.**

## DAY 6

# The Gift of Peace

READ JOHN 14:27-31.

*"Peace I leave with you. My peace I give to you. I do not give to you as the world gives. Don't let your heart be troubled or fearful."*
*— John 14:27*

## DISCOVER

In John 14, Jesus is preparing His disciples for the time when when He will no longer be with them in person. Although He will return to the Father, He won't leave them alone: He promises to give them the Holy Spirit. The Holy Spirit will do many things in their lives, but one of the greatest things He will do is bring them peace.

Imagine being so close to Jesus for several years—leaving everything to follow Him—and then realizing that He would be returning to heaven. The disciples must have been unsettled and worried. But Jesus assured them that they would not be alone. They would have the Holy Spirit.

Jesus doesn't want you to worry about the future. He knows what's ahead, and His Spirit will be with you each step of the way. You can experience peace despite the uncertainties that lie ahead. But that peace does not come from the world. There is nothing in this world that can calm your soul through life's challenges like Jesus. He is the Prince of peace. Don't let your heart be troubled. He will give you the peace to quiet all your fears.

# MEMORY VERSE

**“PEACE I LEAVE WITH YOU. MY PEACE I GIVE TO YOU. I DO NOT GIVE TO YOU AS THE WORLD GIVES. DON’T LET YOUR HEART BE TROUBLED OR FEARFUL.”**

**— JOHN 14:27**

DAY 7

# How to Sleep at Night

READ PROVERBS 19.

*The fear of the* L*ORD leads to life; one will sleep at night without danger.*
*— Proverbs 19:23*

## DISCOVER

When you have the kind of fear of the Lord that is taught in Scripture, it means you will live the right way. Since pleasing and honoring God will be the biggest factor in your decision making, those decisions will create habits and routines that result in a godly and upright life. Of course, living a godly life doesn't mean you won't experience hardships. On the contrary, the Bible shares countless stories of people who lived the right way and still faced many difficulties.

However, living the right way will mostly help you avoid the consequences that come from an immoral lifestyle. Sin often leads to self-inflicted damage—it has real-world consequences. A lifestyle of sin can adversely affect you mentally, physically, socially, emotionally, and financially. God's way is always best. That is what Proverbs teaches us again and again.

Do you desire to lay down each night with a clear conscience, knowing that you have pleased the Lord that day? There is no substitute for the peace that comes from knowing you have obeyed the Lord. Satan will do everything he can to deceive you into believing this isn't true. But he has been a liar from the beginning. God's ways lead to life and peace.

## DELIGHT

**How have you experienced the consequences of sinful choices?**

**How does fearing the Lord help you avoid the consequences of making sinful choices?**

**What are the motivations behind your decisions?**

## DISPLAY

You may be skeptical about the peace that comes from obeying the Lord. But I challenge you to test it out for yourself. Commit to stopping a sin that you feel is no big deal, or work to overcome a bad habit. See the truth of God's Word for yourself. I am confident that you will have more peace living for God than living to please yourself or others.

Where do you need to begin? What would make the biggest difference if you changed it tomorrow? Honestly evaluate how you are living and be willing to make the hard changes. You will sleep better knowing you are living for Jesus.

**Lord, please forgive me for the ways I have lived for myself and not for You. I give You these areas of my life. Your ways are best, and I am committed to following You more eagerly, starting today. In Jesus's name, Amen.**

DAY 8

# He Fights for You

READ DEUTERONOMY 3:21-29.

*"Don't be afraid of them, for the Lord your God fights for you."*
*— Deuteronomy 3:22*

## DISCOVER

Moses had led the people of Israel out of Egypt and through the Red Sea. Then God renewed His covenant with Israel, gave His people the law, and empowered Moses to lead the nation for forty years in the wilderness. But Moses would not be the leader to take them into the Promised Land. God allowed Moses to see it from afar, but He would raise up Joshua to take the people across the Jordan River and into the land.

Imagine how intimidated Joshua must have been. He had been at Moses's side for years, but he had never carried the weight of leading the nation on his own. There would be challenges within and enemies all around. But Moses strengthened Joshua with these words, "Don't be afraid of them, for the Lord your God fights for you" (Deut. 3:22).

The time will come when you no longer have your parents, pastors, or teachers by your side. There will be challenges ahead that they won't be able to walk with you through. But the things you have learned under their leadership have equipped you for those difficult days that lie ahead. Most importantly, the same God who led them will lead you. He will fight for you. Therefore, do not be afraid. Step forward into God's promises today.

## DELIGHT

**Who has made the biggest impact on your faith? Explain.**

**How would you continue forward if the baton of leadership in your team or in your youth group was passed to you?**

**What can you take away from Moses's encouragement to Joshua?**

## DISPLAY

God works in seasons. He develops and prepares us, then He raises us up with opportunities to serve in His kingdom. It is important that you learn all you can from the godly mentors Jesus has put in your life in this season. It is a special time of preparation that you won't get back. Therefore, humbly learn and eagerly serve. One day, it will be your time to lead, and God will be with you in all the battles you face.

**Lord, prepare me, just as You prepared Joshua for the future You planned for him. Help me to overcome the fears and doubts I have. I placed my fears at Your feet and trust You to fight for me. In Jesus's name, Amen.**

DAY 9

# No Fear in Forgiveness

READ 1 JOHN 1:5-10.

*If we confess our sins, he is faithful and righteous to forgive us our sins and to cleanse us from all unrighteousness.*
*— 1 John 1:9*

## DISCOVER

None of us are capable of living sinlessly. Our hope is entirely in Jesus. The apostle John reminds us that the blood of Jesus cleanses us from all sin. Notice that word *all*. There is no sin that Jesus cannot cleanse you from. No matter how bad you think it was, Jesus is able to forgive and heal you.

But there is an important step that we must take to experience that forgiveness. John says that we must confess. It is when we bring our sin into the light, where God is, that the darkness loses its power over us. You can be washed completely. God is faithful to forgive. He is eager to be gracious to you, and will do it every single time. Not only is He faithful; He is also just. Jesus took our judgment, so God's mercy towards us is just.

Do not hesitate or delay. Confess your sins to God and receive His forgiveness. Also, notice how God promises more than a pardon. He is also faithful to cleanse us. God will transform you if you want to forsake your sin to live for Him. Don't settle just for forgiveness: press on to be transformed by the power of Jesus.

## DELIGHT

**What do you need to confess to God?**

**Do you have confidence that He will truly forgive you? Why or why not?**

**How can you move from forgiveness to cleansing?**

## DISPLAY

Confession is not a one-time event—it ought to be a daily habit. Don't let the list grow long; rather, confess your sins as you commit them, one at a time. God has just as much grace and mercy for you as He ever has before. His grace will never run out, so never stop running to Him.

As you consider what you need to confess, try to be as specific as possible. Believe that God has truly forgiven you when you confess, and then take steps to remove that sin from your life. You will never regret a lifestyle of confession and repentance.

**Lord Jesus, thank You for dying for me on the cross. I believe You paid my debt in full. I confess my sins to You today, and I receive Your forgiveness. Cleanse me now of all unrighteousness. Align my heart with Yours regarding my sin. In Jesus's name, Amen.**

**DAY 10**

# Final Victory Over Fear

READ REVELATION 1:9-20.

*When I saw him, I fell at his feet like a dead man. He laid his right hand on me and said, "Don't be afraid. I am the First and the Last, and the Living One. I was dead, but look — I am alive forever and ever, and I hold the keys of death and Hades."*
*— Revelation 1:17-18*

## DISCOVER

The apostle John had a vision of the risen and reigning Jesus—and the Jesus in his vision was unlike the humble Jesus of His earthly ministry. The closest experience to this for John may have been when he saw Jesus on the mount of transfiguration (see Matt. 17:1-13). The person before him in Revelation 1 was the ascended and exalted King of kings.

The presence of the glorified Jesus is overwhelming. He is so mighty that anyone in His presence feels utterly weak. He is so alive and glorious that any person in His presence would feel dead. But the risen and reigning Jesus reached down to John and assured Him, "Fear not." It wasn't because Jesus isn't actually worthy of our fear—He is! But our fears are undone because our awesome God is for us. The only one you must fear is for you.

Jesus holds the keys to eternity, so you can trust Him with the present. Take each step today knowing that He holds you; you are right in His hands. The One who was raised from the dead will also raise you up to live with Him forever. So take heart. Press on. Look up. See Him there in victory. See Him there in power. Know that He is with you. And one day, you will be with Him.

## DELIGHT

**How do these verses reshape your view of Jesus?**

**How does this portrayal of Jesus bring you hope?**

**What does it look like for you to trust Jesus with your present, knowing He holds eternity in His hands?**

## DISPLAY

John's vision of the risen and glorified Jesus ought to bring you boldness in your faith. Jesus suffered and died but was raised and reigns forever. If He can do that, what can't He do for you? When you know He holds the future, you ought to have confidence in obeying Him in your life right now. So think of ways that you can put your faith into action. Take inventory of each area of your life. Are you being controlled by fear or motivated by Jesus? Live confidently knowing that the eternal God is for you and has told you, "Fear not."

**Lord, You are the living God. I believe that You hold eternity in Your hands. Thank You for saving me. You have triumphed over all, and I look to You for victory today. Give me the courage to live for You. In Jesus's name, Amen.**

SECTION 2

# 10 REASONS NOT TO FEAR

*It is one thing to say, "Do not be afraid." It is another thing to provide meaningful evidence for why we don't need to fear. Over the next ten days, we will discover ten reasons that God's Word gives us not to fear.*

DAY 11

# The Lord Is Your Helper

READ ISAIAH 41:8-20.

*For I am the LORD your God, who holds your right hand,*
*who says to you, "Do not fear, I will help you."*
*— Isaiah 41:13*

## DISCOVER

None of us can make it through life on our own strength. We're all human, and if we're honest, we know the limitations of our power and recognize our need for help. As a child of God, your help comes from above. The Lord Himself will come to your aid in your moments of need.

When my children call for my help, they know I will come running to their aid. Why? They are mine and I love them unconditionally. I think of those times when they were learning new things, like roller skating or using a pogo stick. I would hold their hands the whole way. They couldn't do it by themselves, but they didn't need to, because they have a father who will hold them up. And so it is with your heavenly Father.

Look back at Isaiah 41:13. See how personal God's help is. He is the Lord your God. He holds your right hand. He says to you, "Do not fear—I will help you." Even though there are over eight billion people on this planet, God still sees you individually. He is personally committed to you and will help you through whatever you are facing today. Through every season, hear His reassuring words: "Do not fear—I will help you."

## DELIGHT

**In what area of your life do you need God's help the most?**

**How has God helped you in the past?**

**What do you need to do to accept His help?**

## DISPLAY

I am eager to help my children, but sometimes they are less eager to receive my help. When they were toddlers, they wanted to dress themselves, even though they couldn't get their little arms and legs in and out of their clothes. As they grow, that attitude remains—it's just about different things now. But if they would humble themselves, help is available to them.

Sometimes we don't want God's help—we're prideful and want to do it our own way. We know if we turn to God, we will have do it His way. So, we stubbornly march ahead on our own.

But God wants to help you. Turn to your heavenly Father today. Let Him hold your hand and walk with you through this season.

**Heavenly Father, I admit that I need Your help. I do not have the wisdom or strength to walk through this season of my life alone. Thank You for caring for me and helping me in every way. In Jesus's name, Amen.**

DAY 12

# The Lord Will Rescue You

READ PSALM 34.

*I sought the* Lord, *and he answered me and rescued me from all my fears.*
*— Psalm 34:4*

## DISCOVER

David faced constant danger throughout a significant portion of his life. When he wrote this psalm, he was on the run from King Saul, who was seeking to kill him. But God had a purpose for David that could not be destroyed. He led David through this fearful season and rescued him.

In his despair, David went to the Lord. God was his refuge. David didn't seek revenge against Saul. He didn't get bitter or angry. Instead, David walked with integrity and brought his prayers to God for help. God rescued David from the hand of Saul, but He also rescued David from his fears. Through the scariest situations David faced, God gave him joy (see Ps. 34:5,8).

Fear and joy don't mix. They're like oil and water. But when God rescues you from your fears, that place in your heart can be filled with joy, peace, and hope again. The joy isn't dependent upon a change in your situation; God can give you joy and peace before the problem is resolved. I have personally experienced the power of God to overcome my fears, even when the scary situation remains. It happens as we seek the Lord through our pain. Trust in Him and see how He will rescue you from all your fears.

## DELIGHT

**How have your fears often stolen your joy?**

**When have you observed someone experiencing joy even through a scary experience?**

**How can you find that same kind of joy in your life?**

## DISPLAY

David sought the Lord and called out to Him in prayer. Sometimes we forget that it's the simple things we've heard all along that make a big difference. You don't have to reinvent the wheel. It's through the daily spiritual discipline of prayer where we exchange our fears for joy. Lay all your anxieties and fears at Jesus's feet each morning. Do it again and again throughout the day as necessary. Watch how He will rescue you from those fears and fill your heart with joy. Then, you will be singing God's praises as David did in Psalm 34.

**Lord, today I am seeking You as I go through all the situations in my life. It is scary, but I trust You. Please give me joy despite these difficulties so that I can show others Your power in my life. In Jesus's name, Amen.**

DAY 13

# You're Never Abandoned

READ DEUTERONOMY 31:1-8.

*"Be strong and courageous; don't be terrified or afraid of them.*
*For the LORD your God is the one who will go with you;*
*he will not leave you or abandon you."*
*— Deuteronomy 31:6*

## DISCOVER

The people of Israel had Moses as their leader for over forty years. (In America, that is the equivalent of ten consecutive presidential terms!) He was Israel's leader for multiple generations. In these verses, he tells them that he will not be going with them into the Promised Land. But they had no reason for fear. The Lord God would be with them. He would not leave them or abandon them.

They could step into the future without fear because the power was never Moses's to begin with: it was always God's power working *through* Moses to lead the people. God has used many people in your life to lead, protect, and bless you as well. But it has been God's power that has sustained you all along. And He will have just as much power tomorrow as He has today.

People may be a major influence in your life for only a season, but it is God who will be there in every season. He will never leave you. The future is sure to be full of challenges and fears, but do not be afraid. The Lord will go with you every step of the journey. He is with you today and He will be with you always.

## DELIGHT

**Whom has God used in your life to guide you to where you are today? List at least three people.**

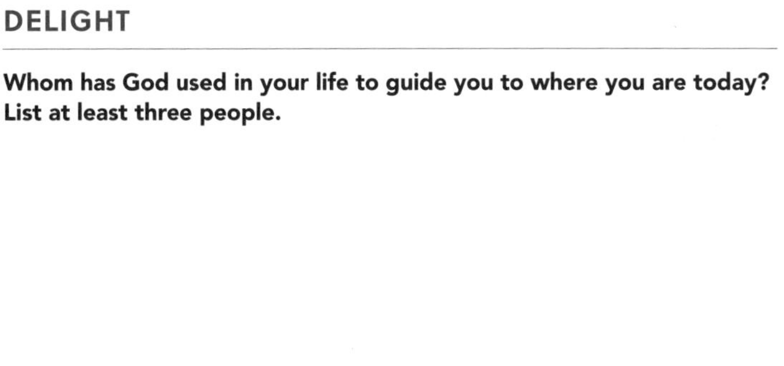

**What fears do you have about the prospect of not having some of those people close to you in the seasons ahead?**

**How can you remind yourself of God's presence and power in your life as you go forward?**

## DISPLAY

The children of Israel had many enemies ahead, and the battles and opposition would be fierce. Maybe you worry about the spiritual battles before you. Perhaps you're nervous to face various kinds of opposition and friction as you live for Jesus. Take a moment to note how God has been there for you in the past. What has He delivered you from? How have you seen Him work in your life? As you recall those things, remember that God is always the same and will be there for you no matter what.

**Lord, thank You for the many ways You have been with me through all the ups and downs. Thank You for the people You have placed in my life in each season. I trust Your power and kindness to be there with me today, tomorrow, and always. In Jesus's name, Amen.**

## DAY 14

# He Is with You

READ JOSHUA 1:1-9.

*"Haven't I commanded you: be strong and courageous? Do not be afraid or discouraged, for the LORD your God is with you wherever you go."*
*— Joshua 1:9*

## DISCOVER

Satan has all kinds of tactics to intimidate you. He wants you to be afraid of so many things, but one of the main things he wants you to fear is what will happen if you go "all in" for Jesus. It's easy to follow Jesus half-heartedly—many people are doing it. You can blend right in. But it takes courage to be sold out for Christ.

God told Joshua to be very strong and courageous, but He wasn't primarily referring to physical strength. God wanted Joshua to courageously obey His commands. There is immense social pressure to ignore God's instructions and live according to the moral compass of the modern world. The risk of being misunderstood, mocked, or even to lose friends is very real. Living for Jesus requires courage.

But when it gets hard, remember God's promise—"Do not be afraid or discouraged, for the LORD your God is with you wherever you go" (Josh. 1:9). It is better to have the approval of God and be rejected by people than to be praised by people but rejected by God. May the Lord give you courage in every circumstance to please Him, and may you always know that He is with you even when the world is against you.

## DAY 15

# You Can Escape the Snare

READ PROVERBS 29.

*The fear of mankind is a snare, but the one who trusts in the LORD is protected.*
*— Proverbs 29:25*

## DISCOVER

A snare is used to trap unsuspecting prey. When an animal is ensnared, it has been tricked into thinking something is safe and good rather than deadly. Proverbs teaches us that the fear of humans is a snare. That means living for the approval of people is dangerous.

You know you are fearing people when your decisions are motivated by how others will respond to you. We should consider others in our decisions, but pleasing people cannot be the number one priority. What pleases one person will displease someone else. Just ask a referee in sports! Unlike the Lord, people are fickle. They change their minds and perspectives all the time. You may be pleasing them one day and upsetting them the next.

When you seek to please people, you are chasing a moving target. That is true at the individual level, but it is even more true culturally. What is approved one decade is condemned the next. What is praised in one generation is shamed in the next. It will never be enough. Instead, look to God's unchanging standards and live to please Him. You can always trust Him, and you never have to worry about Him changing His mind about you. He is the only One worth living for.

## DELIGHT

**Who do you want to please more than anyone else? Why?**

**How do you struggle with the fear of people?**

**In what area do you need to start pleasing God instead of people?**

## DISPLAY

Consider the ways that you try to be a people pleaser. We all struggle with it to varying degrees, so all of us can think of something. Note that your aim should not be to *displease* people for the sake of *not* being a people pleaser. The goal is always to please God, not to displease people. But sometimes pleasing God will frustrate and disappoint people, and that's okay. Talk to someone about the ways you struggle with the fear of people. Ask this person how he or she deals with it, and seek guidance for how to navigate this difficult issue.

**Lord Jesus, I see that people pleasing can be a trap. The temptation is very hard to fight sometimes, so I ask You to help me in this area. I want to please You most of all. Help me please You today. In Jesus's name, Amen.**

**DAY 16**

# You Are Loved Every Day

READ ROMANS 8:31-39.

*For I am persuaded that neither death nor life, nor angels nor rulers, nor things present nor things to come, nor powers, nor height nor depth, nor any other created thing will be able to separate us from the love of God that is in Christ Jesus our Lord.*
*— Romans 8:38-39*

## DISCOVER

You may have heard it a thousand times, but pause to consider the fact that God loves you. How can you know that? The apostle Paul says that we see God's love in Jesus. He did not spare His own Son but gave Him up for our salvation. Jesus's love is also displayed through His constant prayers on our behalf. He is interceding for you.

When you go through difficult times—like the things Paul mentions in these verses—you can be tempted to question God's love. You may ask, *Does God really love me if He is letting me go through all these trials?* The answer here is a resounding "Yes!" Why? Because nothing can separate you from the love of God.

Your circumstances will never be the way to measure God's love for you. God's love is measured in Jesus. He died for you, He forgave you, and He is interceding for you now. In all the fearful situations you may face in life, you never have to fear the loss of God's love. He loves you eternally and unconditionally. God loves you just as much today as He did on the day Jesus died for you. Remember the promise of His love through all of life's ups and downs.

## DELIGHT

**When have you questioned God's love for you?**

**What helps you know that God truly loves you?**

**Why is it important to remember God's love in your trials?**

## DISPLAY

We must fight our doubts about God's love with the truth of the gospel. This world is full of painful experiences that cause us to question the love of God. When that happens, we must remind ourselves of all that Jesus did to save us. Also, remember the Father's love for Jesus. The Father and Son love each other perfectly, but that doesn't mean Jesus had an easy life. The same was true of the disciples as well as many other people in the Bible. Memorize Romans 8:38-39 over the next week. Internalize these words by planting them in your heart and mind so that you can recall them in the moment you need them most.

**Heavenly Father, I believe You love me perfectly and unconditionally. No matter what I face, I can trust Your love for me. Help me never forget Your love. In Jesus's name, Amen.**

# MEMORY VERSES

**For I am persuaded that neither death nor life, nor angels nor rulers, nor things present nor things to come, nor powers, nor height nor depth, nor any other created thing will be able to separate us from the love of God that is in Christ Jesus our Lord.**

— Romans 8:38–39

**DAY 17**

# You Are His

READ ISAIAH 43:1-7.

*Now this is what the LORD says — the one who created you, Jacob, and the one who formed you, Israel — "Do not fear, for I have redeemed you; I have called you by your name; you are mine."*
*— Isaiah 43:1*

## DISCOVER

One of my daughters loves to make little bracelets for herself and her friends. She thinks through each detail, carefully selecting the colors and patterns. When she finishes a bracelet, it becomes very special to her. Why? Because she made it. If my daughter cares that much about a bracelet, how much more special must you be to God?

In Isaiah 43, the Lord reminds the people of Israel that He created them. Not only did He make them, God also named them. He set them apart. He rescued them out of Egypt and made them His special people. For all who belong to Jesus, God has done the same thing. God has done more than just create you. That alone is enough for Him to care for you, but He has taken it even further. God has redeemed you and called you by name.

Of course, there would be fearful things ahead for the people of Israel. They would have to "pass through the waters" and "walk through the fire" (Isa. 43:2). But in all of it, God would be with them. He would not forget His own people, and He will not forget you. Fear not, for He has redeemed you; He has called you by name. You are His.

## DELIGHT

**What did God do to redeem you?**

**When did God call you by name to become His child?**

**How can you face whatever comes next, knowing you are His?**

## DISPLAY

Think of all the things that you have that are special to you. Make a list. Consider collecting them into one spot and pondering why you love them. We all have special possessions—personally visualizing the things you care about could be a helpful exercise as you consider the fact that you are God's special possession.

Why are those things special to you? Did you make any of them? Did you purchase them yourself? Do they have special worth to you? You are all of those things and more to God! He made you, purchased you, and has given you immeasurable worth. He will not forsake you, whom He cares so deeply for.

**Lord, I belong to You. You are my Creator, Redeemer, and Father. Cover me in the peace that comes from knowing that I am Yours. Walk with me through the challenges that I will face today. In Jesus's name, Amen.**

## DAY 18

# You Can Find Joy

READ PSALM 94.

*If I say, "My foot is slipping," your faithful love will support me, Lord. When I am filled with cares, your comfort brings me joy.*
*— Psalm 94:18-19*

## DISCOVER

Psalm 94 describes the experience of a believer who is in the middle of an unjust society—a place that calls evil good and persecutes the righteous. The psalmist reminds us that God is faithful and true. He will support us even in wicked times.

The psalmist felt as if he was on the brink of falling. Like someone walking on ice, he felt his feet about to slip. But the Lord was there to catch him and keep him from falling. In verse 19, he moves from the illustration to the actual experience in his heart. He says, "When I am filled with cares, your comfort brings me joy" (Ps. 94:19). The cares of life were piling up on him. His heart was filled with angst, but the Lord comforted him. God's comfort moved him from worry to joy.

Do you sometimes feel yourself slipping? You may be slipping mentally or emotionally. You may be filled with many cares. God is able to exchange those sorrows for many joys. Take heart, for God is a refuge (see Ps. 94:22). He is a rock of protection, and He will judge the wicked and deal with His people justly (see Ps. 94:22-23).

## DELIGHT

**What are the cares that fill your heart and mind?**

**How do you try to deal with those worries?**

**What can you do to stand on emotionally stable ground?**

## DISPLAY

The psalmist recognized that he was in danger of slipping—he wasn't in denial about the reality of his situation. That is the first step to standing on solid ground. God will support and comfort you through every struggle. It is critical that you are turning to Him and not trying to walk the path alone. God has put people in your life to whom you can talk about your worries and cares. Don't delay—go to someone today if you're struggling. Then, find refuge in the Lord and experience the joy of His support in a dark and difficult world.

**Lord, I humbly acknowledge that I could slip on my own. I need You to hold me up and give me stability me through uncertain times. Exchange my fears for joy and place my feet on a firm foundation. In Jesus's name, Amen.**

## DAY 19

# You Are Blessed

READ 1 PETER 3:13-17.

*But even if you should suffer for righteousness, you are blessed. Do not fear them or be intimidated.*
*— 1 Peter 3:14*

## DISCOVER

Virtually every product you can buy comes with a warning label. This is especially true of medicine. Although it's a great blessing to have access to modern medicine, taking medication often has side effects that are less desirable. But usually, we take the medicine anyway, because the benefit outweighs the side effects. The same is true of living for Jesus. It is a great blessing, but it may also result in some unwanted side effects. Regardless, we live for Jesus.

Living righteously may result in suffering. Now, there's a kind of suffering that's a natural result of sin. When we do the wrong thing, we experience painful and difficult consequences. But what about when we do right? In this fallen world, that too may result in suffering. This kind of suffering is the unnatural result of doing good, and it can take the form of feeling like a social outcast or even experiencing persecution.

But Peter reminds us not to be afraid or intimidated by people. Rather, remember how blessed you are to belong to God. In the present, we may be grieved by various trials (see 1 Pet. 1:6). But "the God of all grace, who called you to his eternal glory in Christ, will himself restore, establish, strengthen, and support you after you have suffered a little while" (1 Pet. 5:10). Therefore, continue to do what is right, knowing it will be worth it for all of eternity.

## DELIGHT

**What "side effects" have you experienced while following Jesus?**

**How have you felt intimidated to live out your faith?**

**How does it encourage you to remember that you are blessed despite the challenges of living for Jesus?**

## DISPLAY

Peter tells us that we are blessed to be Christians. Write down the ways that it is a blessing to be a follower of Jesus. These blessings may relate to the present or eternity, and they may be physical, spiritual, relational, or emotional. Regardless of what blessings you think of, the goal is to realize the amazing privilege it is to belong to Christ.

In moments when you feel afraid or intimidated to live out your faith, refer to this list of blessings as motivation to do what you know is right. Understand that it won't be easy. It wasn't easy for the Christians who came before us, and it won't be easy now. But for all of eternity, you will never regret living your life for Christ.

**Lord, when following You feels scary, remind me of the many blessings I have in You. Grow my gratitude and shrink my fears. Thank You for every way that You have blessed me. In Jesus's name, Amen.**

**DAY 20**

# You Can Honor Everyone

READ 1 PETER 2:11-17.

*Honor everyone. Love the brothers and sisters.*
*Fear God. Honor the emperor.*
*— 1 Peter 2:17*

## DISCOVER

We have seen how Scripture teaches us to fear the Lord. We have also learned a lot about the dangers of fearing people. In these verses, the apostle Peter puts all of the human and divine relationships in their proper place.

We ought to honor everyone. All people should be treated honorably, because they, too, are made in the image of God. (And, by the way, you can treat someone with honor and not agree with her or him on everything!) We also ought to love other believers. We are a spiritual family, and there should be a special love that exist in our hearts for our brothers and sisters in Christ. We should fear God because He alone deserves our highest reverence and devotion. Finally, we should honor our leaders out of respect for their authority.

So many of the problems we face relationally happen because we get these things out of order—or even worse, we ignore these instructions altogether. We disrespect authorities, mistreat people who are different from us, and fail to love one another in the church. The root problem is that we do not fear God. If we get that relationship right, the others will follow. Until then, we will likely struggle to relate to other people the way God wants us to. We will act out of fear rather than out of love and honor. May God change our hearts in a way that transforms our relationships for His glory.

## DELIGHT

**What would it look like for you to treat all people honorably?**

**How can you love other Christians better?**

**How can you honor people in authority more?**

## DISPLAY

Take another look at the categories listed in 1 Peter 2:17, and try to identify the weakest area of relationships for you out of these categories. Think of ways that you can improve in that area. You may be struggling most in a specific relationship, such as with an authority figure in your life. Be specific in your application. Take steps to improve that relationship which is most fractured and broken.

God cares about how we treat other people because our personal, human relationships are reflections of our relationship with Him. We want other people to glorify our Father in heaven as a result of our lives. Put God's Word into action this week in every category of relationship in your life.

**Lord, I want to live in a way that brings You glory. I know my relationships are a big part of that, so I ask that You help me relate to people in the right way. In Jesus's name, Amen.**

SECTION 3

# 10 WAYS TO FIGHT FEAR

*It is not enough to just read God's Word—we must apply His Word for it to have the most powerful effect in our lives. The Scriptures show us how to respond to our fears in a variety of situations. Over the next ten days, we will learn ten ways the Bible teaches us to fight fear.*

## DAY 21

# Trust in the Lord

READ PSALM 56.

*When I am afraid, I will trust in you. In God, whose word I praise, in God I trust; I will not be afraid. What can mere mortals do to me?*
*— Psalm 56:3-4*

## DISCOVER

David had been mistreated by the Philistines. In Psalm 56, he is crying out to God to fight on his behalf against these enemies. This psalm is not a completed testimony, where David is looking back at how God delivered him. Instead, David wrote this psalm from right in the middle of his struggle.

Scriptures like this give us a glimpse into the hearts and minds of believers who have come before us and the way they handled trials. They teach us how to respond when our story is yet to be complete. In this psalm, we learn that trust was the antidote to David's fear. Even though the dangers remained, he trusted God with his life. He said, "What can mere mortals do to me?" (Ps. 56:4) If you're anything like me you may be thinking, "A lot! They can kill you, David!"

But David understood that nothing could happen to him that was outside of God's control. He trusted God and knew God was for him (see Ps. 56:9). As Jesus said, "Don't fear those who kill the body but are not able to kill the soul . . . . Aren't two sparrows sold for a penny? Yet not one of them falls to the ground without your Father's consent. But even the hairs of your head have all been counted" (Matt. 10:28-30). If the Lord knows how many hairs you have and has concern for each of them, then you can trust Him with everything else.

## DELIGHT

**What do you do when you are afraid?**

**How can you trust God as you go through trials?**

**Who are some people you can learn from who've trusted God through the trials of their lives?**

## DISPLAY

David trusted God because he believed God's Word. He said, "I will trust in you. In God, whose word I praise" (Ps. 56:3-4). You will not trust in God if you don't trust His Word. As in any other relationship, trust is essential. When someone shows faithfulness and truthfulness, your trust in that person grows. Well, God has shown Himself to be faithful and true through many generations. We have so many stories in the Bible that demonstrate that our God is trustworthy. Take some time to look up at least three stories in Scripture where God was faithful to people through their trials. Remember: what God has done for others will grow your trust in Him for your own life. To start with, check out 1 Samuel 21:10-15 to see the situation that inspired David to write Psalm 56.

**Lord, help me to trust You with every situation I face today. You have always been faithful to Your people, and I know You will do the same for me. Thank You for remaining faithful to me. In Jesus's name, Amen.**

DAY 22

# Pray and Obey

READ PHILIPPIANS 4:4-9.

*Don't worry about anything, but in everything, through prayer and petition with thanksgiving, present your requests to God.*
*— Philippians 4:6*

## DISCOVER

Paul wrote this letter to the church at Philippi from prison. He knew all about the fears that can arise in life. But he didn't let those fears control his life, and he did not want the believers at Philippi to be crippled by fear or worry, either.

So Paul gave them clear action steps to take to deal with their fears and worries: prayer, thanksgiving, a good mindset, and imitating godliness. In prayer, we lay our fears and worries at Jesus's feet. Through thanksgiving, we remind our souls of God's goodness and kindness. With the right mindset, we focus our attention on the things that promote joy and peace. And as we imitate the godly example of others, we experience God's peace and presence in our lives (see Phil. 4:9).

As you go through various difficulties, try to implement this strategy for yourself. Pray, focus on the good, and then keep doing what is right. Be so preoccupied with doing good that you hardly have time to worry about anything. God will surround you with peace as you focus on the things you can control. It's just as Jesus said in the Sermon on the Mount: "Seek first the kingdom of God and his righteousness, and all these things will be provided for you" (Matt. 6:33).

## DELIGHT

**How do you respond to worry on most days?**

**How can you take the initiative against worry right in the moment?**

**Why is it important to be busy doing good even through hard times?**

## DISPLAY

We are bombarded with a lot of negativity in our world. People complain and stress out in our families, at school, at church, and beyond. There's a constant stream of toxic thinking on our phones and plenty of panic in the news. It is critical, then, to actively focus on what is true, honorable, pure, and lovely. This is not a passive mindset. The default is worry and negativity—so consider the practical ways you can get your mind in the right place each day. This is a moment by moment battle, but Jesus can give you the victory. Below, write down two or three ways you can get your mind in the right place each day, regardless of what other emotions and factors are around you.

**Lord, I set my mind on You today. Take control of my thoughts and protect me from worry and fear. Please walk with me and allow me to sense Your presence as I live for You. Help me focus on You. In Jesus's name, Amen.**

DAY 23

# Fear Is Not from God

READ 2 TIMOTHY 1:7-12.

*For God has not given us a spirit of fear,*
*but one of power, love, and sound judgment.*
*— 2 Timothy 1:7*

## DISCOVER

In this letter, the apostle Paul was writing to Timothy, his friend and mentee. Timothy was pastoring the church in Ephesus, and this letter was meant to encourage him in his ministry and leadership. Timothy may have been timid and nervous as a young leader without his mentor present anymore. But Paul reminded him that God did not give him a spirit of fear. God gave Timothy a spirit of power, love, and sound judgment.

Consider how fear undermines these things. Fear steals our strength. Fear ignites our self-preservation and defensiveness. It is difficult to love people well when you see them as threats. You won't love selflessly when you are constantly afraid in your relationships. Fear also tends to make us irrational. We don't exercise sound judgment when we are controlled by fear.

Fear is not from God. Rather, God has given you spiritual power. He has poured His Spirit into your heart. Through Him, you can love others and walk in wisdom. Don't let fear steal what God has given you. He has called you by His grace, saved you through Jesus, and will guard you through life's many challenges.

## DELIGHT

**How does fear affect your personality and actions?**

**Why is it important to understand that fear affects things like your capacity for love and wisdom?**

**What are steps you can take to grow in love and wisdom?**

## DELIGHT

**What are you waiting on God for?**

**What are you doing while you wait?**

**How can you serve Him while you wait?**

## DISPLAY

I have heard many preachers describe waiting on the Lord like waiting a table at a restaurant. The wait staff aren't sitting in the kitchen twiddling their thumbs. They're busy serving. Likewise, waiting for the Lord isn't passive—it's the time to press on in doing good. If we fail to serve the Lord in our waiting, we won't be ready when He does show up. For example, think of a future job or relationship that God may bring into your life. If you aren't developing as a person in this season, you won't be who you need to be when those opportunities come. So as you wait, seek and serve the Lord with all your heart. Think about one way you can serve the Lord this week in your home, church, school, or an activity you're involved in. Write your thoughts below.

**Lord, You are the one who controls my future. I don't know when or how You will show up, but I am trusting that Your plans are good for me. In the meantime, help me to serve You faithfully in each season. In Jesus's name, Amen.**

DAY 25

# The Trap of Pride

READ 1 PETER 5:6-11.

*Humble yourselves, therefore, under the mighty hand of God, so that he may exalt you at the proper time, casting all your cares on him, because he cares about you.*
*— 1 Peter 5:6-7*

## DISCOVER

Satan will kick you while you are down. The believers in 1 Peter were already experiencing various kinds of suffering (see 1 Pet. 5:9). But Satan was still seeking ways to harm them (see 1 Pet. 5:8). The same will often be true for us as well. Satan wants to destroy us, but God has shown us how to overcome him.

Peter tells us to humble ourselves. Satan wants to puff you up with pride because pride is one of the primary ways he can bring you down. Satan knows our weaknesses, but he's no match for God. So humble yourself before God.

Peter also tells us to cast our cares upon the Lord. That means we can be honest about our worries and fears. God loves you and cares for you, so you can tell Him the truth.

Pride and prayer don't mix. When we're being prideful, we don't want to be real with God or with others about our struggles. We put on a face and pretend we're doing better than we really are. It's a dangerous game to play. Satan uses our pride to trap us. But when we humbly acknowledge our need for the Lord and cast our cares on Him, we will experience peace in many kinds of trials.

## DELIGHT

**What cares do you need to turn over to God?**

**How does pride hinder your prayer life?**

**What can you do to resist Satan this week?**

## DISPLAY

Pride will wreck your life far more than trials alone will. God can use your trials to stretch your faith, but God doesn't use our pride. To the contrary: pride disrupts our relationship with God and gives Satan an open door in our lives. Humility is critical to your spiritual health. Try to identify some areas where you struggle with pride. It may be scary to face, but cast those cares upon the Lord and trust that He can do more with your humility than you could ever do in your own pride.

**Lord, I confess my pride to You. Help me to humble myself and depend on You. I give You all my cares today. Thank You for all the ways You care for me. In Jesus's name, Amen.**

## DAY 26

# He Is Our Refuge

READ PSALM 118.

*It is better to take refuge in the LORD than to trust in humanity.*
*— Psalm 118:8*

## DISCOVER

Who are you hoping in? We often say that our hope is in God, but do our actions reflect that? When you look around, it seems like so many people are hoping in money, pleasure, entertainment, politics, material possessions—anything other than God. They take refuge from life's storms by escaping reality through entertainment or by putting their hope in other people.

It is one thing to look around at others, but it is a much harder thing to look in the mirror. If we're honest with ourselves, we all let people down. This is why David challenges us to take refuge in the Lord. People are inconsistent. Even when they have the best intentions, they can still let you down. God is our only trustworthy refuge in all circumstances.

The psalmist gives us several reasons to trust in God as our refuge: His faithful love endures forever (see Ps. 118:2); He answers our prayers (see Ps. 118:5); He is for us and helps us (see Ps. 118:6-7). Psalm 118 warns us not to trust in nobles—even the most powerful people on earth cannot be our refuge! God is the only One is who all powerful. Others may reject Jesus, but He is the stone the builders rejected, our cornerstone (see Ps. 118:22). He is a refuge like no other. Trust in Him today.

## DELIGHT

**Why do you need to take refuge in God?**

**How has God shown His faithful love to you in the past?**

**What can you do to build your hope in Him?**

## DISPLAY

This psalm is a reminder of God's character. It is God's perfect character that makes Him the greatest refuge in times of trouble. Make a list of all the reasons that God is a refuge. List the characteristics of God that stand out to you above people and the other things we tend to hope in. At the same time, consider how other things can let you down. We often seek safety in things that offer no protection in the storms of life. Be honest with yourself about the things you are truly hoping in. When the storms of life come, you will be glad you took refuge in the Lord.

**Lord, I look to You today above every other person and thing. You are faithful and trustworthy. You are my refuge through all of life's storms. Thank You for being a perfect God who loves us so well. In Jesus's name, Amen.**

# MEMORY VERSE